ICONS

SEASIDE STYLE
VOL. II

SEASIDE

Exteriors   Interiors

STYLE

Details

EDITOR **Angelika Taschen**

VOL. II

TASCHEN

HONG KONG KÖLN LONDON LOS ANGELES MADRID PARIS TOKYO

Front Cover: Architect Georges Evripiotis built the Angelopoulos' house on terraces on the coast of Mykonos.
Couverture: L'architecte Georges Evripiotis a construit la maison des Angelopoulos sur des terrasses sur la côte de Mykonos.
Umschlagvorderseite: Das Haus der Angelopoulos baute Architekt Georges Evripiotis auf Terrassen an der Küste von Mykonos.

Back Cover: From Eero Aarnio's "Bubble Chair" there is a view of the sea at Warrnambool in Australia.
Dos de Couverture: Assis dans la « Bubble Chair » d'Eero Aarnio, on regarde la mer à Warrnambool en Australie.
Umschlagrückseite: Im »Bubble Chair« von Eero Aarnio genießt man den Meerblick bei Warrnambool in Australien.

Also available from TASCHEN:

New Seaside Interiors
Hardcover, 24 x 31.6 cm, 300 pages
ISBN 978-3-8365-0387-7 (Edition with English and German cover)
ISBN 978-3-8365-0477-5 (Edition with French cover)

To stay informed about upcoming TASCHEN titles, please request our magazine
at www.taschen.com/magazine or write to TASCHEN, Hohenzollernring 53, D-50672 Cologne,
Germany, contact@taschen.com, Fax: +49-221-254919. We will be happy to send you
a free copy of our magazine which is filled with information about all of our books.

© 2009 TASCHEN GmbH
Hohenzollernring 53, D-50672 Köln
www.taschen.com

© 2009 VG Bild-Kunst, Bonn for the works of Harry Bertoia, Robert Indiana, Grete Jalk,
Charlotte Perriand, Arne Haugen Sørensen, Frank Stella.
© 2009 for the works of Charles and Ray Eames: Eames Office, Venice, CA, www.eamesoffice.com.

Concept, layout and editing by Angelika Taschen, Berlin
General project management by Stephanie Paas, Cologne
Texts by Christiane Reiter, Hamburg
Lithography by Thomas Grell, Cologne
English translation by John Sykes, Cologne
French translation by Michèle Schreyer, Cologne

Printed in Italy
ISBN 978-3-8365-1507-8

CONTENTS SOMMAIRE INHALT

It covers more than 70 per cent of the earth's surface and borders a great variety of coasts on different continents. It produces food and oxygen, healing salts and algae, and dominates the way of life and the economy of many regions. Its moon-governed tides, unfathomable depths and constantly changing moods and colours fascinate us. The sea is a phenomenon – and one of the great subjects of the arts. Legendary books and poems such as Hemingway's "The Old Man and the Sea" and Baudelaire's "Man and the Sea" are devoted to it. The sea inspired Mendelssohn to compose his overture "The Hebrides" and was celebrated in sound with Debussy's "La Mer". In the sea, painters from Caspar David Friedrich and J. M. W. Turner to Ludwig Kirchner and Emil Nolde found the light and the motifs for important works. Architects, too, fall under the attraction of the sea: they turn

HOMAGE TO THE SEA

Elle couvre plus de 70 pour cent de la superficie du globe et jouxte les continents les plus divers. Elle produit de l'oxygène et des aliments, contient des substances aux propriétés thérapeutiques comme le sel et les algues, marque de son empreinte les coutumes et l'économie de nombreuses régions. Ses marées provoquées par la lune, ses profondeurs insondables, ses humeurs et ses teintes changeantes nous fascinent. Mais au-delà des phénomènes naturels que nous observons, la mer est aussi l'un des thèmes majeurs de l'art. Des livres mythiques et des poèmes l'évoquent, qu'il s'agisse du « Vieil homme et la mer » d'Hemingway ou de « L'homme et la Mer » de Baudelaire. Mendelssohn s'est inspiré d'elle pour composer « Les Hébrides » ; Debussy lui a dressé un monument musical avec « La Mer ». De Caspar David Friedrich, Ludwig Kirchner et Emil Nolde à William Turner, des peintres ont trouvé en elle la lumière et les motifs qu'ils recherchaient, créant des œuvres majeures. Quant aux

Es bedeckt mehr als 70 Prozent der Erdoberfläche und grenzt an die unterschiedlichsten Küsten der Kontinente. Es produziert Nahrung und Sauerstoff, heilt mit Wirkstoffen aus Salz und Algen, prägt Brauchtum und Wirtschaft vieler Regionen. Es fasziniert mit seinen vom Mond gelenkten Gezeiten, mit unergründlichen Tiefen und ständig wechselnden Stimmungen sowie Farben. Das Meer ist ein Phänomen – und eines der großen Themen der Künste. Von seinem Wesen erzählen legendäre Bücher und Gedichte wie Hemingways »Der alte Mann und das Meer« oder Baudelaires »Der Mensch und das Meer«. Mendelssohn ließ sich von ihm zu seiner Komposition »Die Hebriden« inspirieren; Debussy setzte ihm mit »La mer« ein Denkmal aus Klängen. Maler fanden an der See das Licht und die Motive für wichtige Werke – von Caspar David Friedrich, Ludwig Kirchner und Emil Nolde bis zu William Turner. Auch vor Architekten macht die Anziehungskraft des Ozeans nicht halt: Sie lassen den

the dream of living by the sea into reality, for themselves and their clients. For some years now, more and more home owners have been choosing famous architects and designers who apply their know-how and powers of empathy to create a residence on the cliffs of Mykonos, a summer house in the dunes of the Hamptons or a villa on the beach in Brazil. The style can be highly sophisticated, glamorous or eccentric, but many interiors have a timeless or relatively simple appearance and make use of natural materials and the classic colour combination of blue and white. Lovers of the sea who create their home themselves on a modest budget also follow these principles, though perhaps less consciously. And a simple wooden hut beneath palm trees or a fisherman's cottage decorated with shells, sea stars and ropes can be a private paradise – and pay homage to the sea and its magic.

architectes, ils sont eux aussi sous le charme et réalisent le rêve d'habitation en bord de mer – pour eux-mêmes et leurs commanditaires. Depuis quelques années, ils sont de plus en plus nombreux à choisir des architectes et des designers de renom qui concevront en experts et avec sensibilité leur propriété sur la côte abrupte de Mykonos, leur maison d'été dans les dunes de Hampton ou leur villa sur la plage brésilienne. Le style de l'habitation peut être très sophistiqué, glamour ou excentrique, mais de nombreux intérieurs sont aussi hors du temps et relativement sobres, misant sur des matériaux naturels et la gamme de coloris classique bleu et blanc. Les amoureux de la mer qui conçoivent eux-mêmes leur foyer avec un budget plus modeste suivent les mêmes principes, mais peut-être moins consciemment. Et la cabane en bois sous les palmiers ou la petite maison de pêcheur décorée de coquillages, d'étoiles de mer et de cordages est un paradis privé, un hommage à la mer et sa magie.

Traum, am Meer zu wohnen, Wirklichkeit werden – für sich selbst und für ihre Auftraggeber. Seit einigen Jahren entscheiden sich immer mehr Hausbesitzer für renommierte Architekten und Designer, die Anwesen wie das an der Steilküste von Mykonos, das Sommerhaus in den Dünen der Hamptons oder die Villa am Strand von Brasilien mit Fachkenntnis und Einfühlungsvermögen entwerfen. Dabei kann der Stil sehr sophisticated, glamourös oder exzentrisch sein – viele Interieurs geben sich aber auch zeitlos und vergleichsweise schlicht, setzen auf natürliche Materialien sowie die klassische Farbkombination Blau-Weiß. Meeresliebhaber, die ihr Haus mit kleinerem Budget selbst gestalten, folgen solchen Prinzipien ebenfalls, nur vielleicht unbewusster. Und auch eine simple Holzhütte unter Palmen oder ein mit Muscheln, Seesternen und Tauen dekoriertes Fischerhäuschen sind ein privates Paradies und eine Hommage – an das Meer und seine Magie.

"He always thought of the sea as la mar, which is what people call her in Spanish when they love her…"

Ernest Hemingway, *The Old Man and the Sea*

« *Il appelait l'océan la mar, qui est le nom que les gens lui donnent en espagnol quand ils l'aiment…* »

Ernest Hemingway, *Le vieil homme et la mer*

»*Er dachte an die See immer als an la mar, so nennt man sie auf Spanisch, wenn man sie liebt …*«

Ernest Hemingway, *Der alte Mann und das Meer*

EXTERIORS

Extérieurs   Aussichten

10/11 On the north coast of Iceland the views of the Eyjafjordur fjord are endless. *Sur la côte du nord de l'Islande, une vue imprenable sur le fjord Eyjafjordur.* An Islands Nordküste eröffnen sich endlos weite Aussichten auf den Fjord Eyjafjordur.

12/13 The house by Todd Saunders and Tommie Wilhelmsen is 80 metres above a fjord. *La maison de Todd Saunders et Tommie Wilhelmsen trône 80 mètres au-dessus d'un fjord.* Das Haus von Todd Saunders und Tommie Wilhelmsen ist 80 Meter über einem Fjord.

14/15 From her terrace the Danish architect Hanne Kjærholm can look out over the Øresund. *De sa terrasse, l'architecte danoise Hanne Kjærholm peut contempler le détroit du Sund.* Von ihrer Terrasse aus überblickt die dänische Architektin Hanne Kjærholm den Øresund.

16/17 View from the apartment designed by Vincent van Duysen in Knokke-Zoute. *Vue depuis l'appartement conçu par Vincent van Duysen à Knokke-Zoute.* Blick aus dem von Vincent van Duysen entworfenen Apartment in Knokke-Zoute.

18/19 Pierre Cardins "Anthénéa" was designed by Jean-Michel Ducancelle. *L'« Anthénéa » de Pierre Cardin a été conçue par Jean-Michel Ducancelle.* Pierre Cardins »Anthénéa« entwarf Jean-Michel Ducancelle.

20/21 Breathtaking view from Fiona Swarovski's villa on Capri. *Superbe vue depuis la villa de Fiona Swarovski à Capri.* Atemberaubender Ausblick von Fiona Swarovskis Villa auf Capri.

22/23 The sun terrace of a villa in Positano, designed by Claudio Lazzarini and Carl Pickering. *La plate-forme solaire d'une villa conçue par Claudio Lazzarini et Carl Pickering à Positano.* Die Sonnenplattform einer von Claudio Lazzarini und Carl Pickering entworfenen Villa in Positano.

24/25 Georges Evripiotis was the designer of Gianna and Theodore Angelopoulos' infinity pool. *La piscine à débordement de Gianna et Theodore Angelopoulos est signée Georges Evripiotis.* Den Infinity-Pool von Gianna und Theodore Angelopoulos entwarf Georges Evripiotis.

26/27 Belquis Zahir used Afghani items to give her terrace on Filicudi an Oriental touch. *Des objets afghans donnent un petit air oriental à la terrasse de Belquis Zahir à Filicudi.* Belquis Zahir verlieh ihrer Terrasse auf Filicudi mit afghanischen Objekten orientalisches Flair.

28/29 Zahir had this shady veranda made from wooden beams and woven cane. *Zahir a fait réaliser à l'aide de poutres et de cannage un avant-toit qui donne de l'ombre.* Das Schatten spendende Vordach ließ Zahir aus Holzbalken und Rohrgeflecht anfertigen.

30/31 Paul Barthelemy preserved the rustic charm of his house on Alicudi in Italy. *Paul Barthelemy a su conserver le charme rustique de sa maison d'Alicudi en Italie.* Paul Barthelemy erhielt den bäuerlichen Charme seines Hauses auf Alicudi in Italien.

32/33 The blue door leads into Christina von Rosen's little fisherman's house on the Algarve. *On entre par la porte bleue dans la petite maison de pêcheur de Christina von Rosen en Algarve.* Durch die blaue Tür betritt man Christina von Rosens kleines Fischerhaus an der Algarve.

34/35 Paul Barthelemy brought the green table to Alicudi from his parents' house in Sicily. *Paul Barthelemy a apporté à Alicudi la table verte de la maison de ses parents en Sicile.* Den grünen Tisch brachte Paul Barthelemy aus seinem Elternhaus in Sizilien nach Alicudi.

36/37 Isay Weinfeld built this house in Iporanga, Brazil, in the form of two cuboids. *Isay Weinfeld a créé cette maison d'Iporanga, au Brésil, à partir de deux cubes.* Isay Weinfeld entwarf dieses Haus aus zwei weißen Kuben im brasilianischen Iporanga.

38/39 Thanks to the sanded floor, the tent-like outdoor area has the feel of a private beach. *Avec son sol de sable, l'espace extérieur aux airs de tente ressemble à une plage privée de luxe.* Dank des Sandbodens wirkt der zeltähnliche Außenbereich wie ein exklusiver Privatstrand.

40/41 The house of fashion designer Lisa Perry in the Hamptons with its modern art. *L'art moderne attire les regards sur la maison de la dessinatrice de mode Lisa Perry à Hampton.* Moderne Kunst macht das Haus von Modedesignerin Lisa Perry in den Hamptons zum Blickfang.

42/43 A table by Robert Indiana and sofas by Alexia Kondylis make the terrace colourful. *Une table de Robert Indiana et des canapés d'Alexia Kondylis mettent de la couleur sur la terrasse.* Ein Tisch von Robert Indiana und Sofas von Alexia Kondylis sorgen auf der Terrasse für Farbe.

44/45 Alan Wanzenberg is the owner of the symmetrically planned Ocean House on Fire Island. *À Fire Island, Alan Wanzenberg possède Ocean House aux lignes symétriques.* Auf Fire Island besitzt Alan Wanzenberg das symmetrisch angelegte Ocean House.

46/47 Mark Ferguson designed this house on Martha's Vineyard in the island's style. *La maison de Martha's Vineyard a été conçue par Mark Ferguson dans le style de l'île.* Das Haus auf Martha's Vineyard entwarf Mark Ferguson im Stil der Insel.

48/49 The bays on the Caribbean coast of Costa Rica still have an untouched appearance. *Les baies semblent encore vierges sur la côte caraïbe du Costa Rica.* An der karibischen Küste von Costa Rica wirken die Buchten noch wie unberührt.

50/51 Daan Nelemans built his wooden house very close to the beach but still right in the jungle. *Daan Nelemans a construit sa maison de bois en pleine jungle mais la plage n'est pas loin.* Ganz nah am Strand und zugleich mitten im Dschungel baute Daan Nelemans sein Holzhaus.

52/53 Mima and César Reyes' house in Puerto Rico was designed by Jorge Pardo. *La maison de Mima et César Reyes à Puerto Rico a été conçue par Jorge Pardo.* Das Haus von Mima und César Reyes in Puerto Rico entwarf Jorge Pardo.

54/55 Azul García Uriburu built her symmetrical house on the beach in Uruguay. *Azul García Uriburu a placé sa maison aux lignes symétriques sur la plage de l'Uruguay.* Azul García Uriburu errichtete ihr symmetrisch angelegtes Haus am Strand von Uruguay.

56/57 The wooden furniture on the shady terrace was designed by Isabelle Firmin Didot. *Les meubles en bois, à l'ombre sur la terrasse, sont signés Isabelle Firmin Didot.* Die Holzmöbel auf der schattigen Terrasse sind Entwürfe von Isabelle Firmin Didot.

58/59 The platfrom of Ken Crosson's house in New Zealand can be raised. *La plate-forme de la maison de Ken Crosson en Nouvelle-Zélande se lève.* Die Plattform von Ken Crossons Haus in Neuseeland kann hochgezogen werden.

60/61 Crosson lives on the Coromandel Peninsula, 20 kilometres from the nearest town. *Crosson vit sur la péninsule de Coromandel ; la prochaine ville est à vingt kilomètres.* Crosson lebt auf der Coromandel-Halbinsel, 20 Kilometer von der nächsten Stadt entfernt.

"At the seaside all is narrow horizontals, the world reduced to a few long straight lines pressed between earth and sky…"

John Banville, *The Sea*

« À la mer, tout est fait d'étroites horizontales, le monde entier se réduit à quelques lignes longues, droites, coincées entre le ciel et la terre…»

John Banville, *La mer*

»An der See besteht alles aus schmalen Waagerechten, die ganze Welt reduziert sich auf ein paar lange, gerade, zwischen Himmel und Erde gezwängte Linien …«

John Banville, *Die See*

INTERIORS

Intérieurs   Einsichten

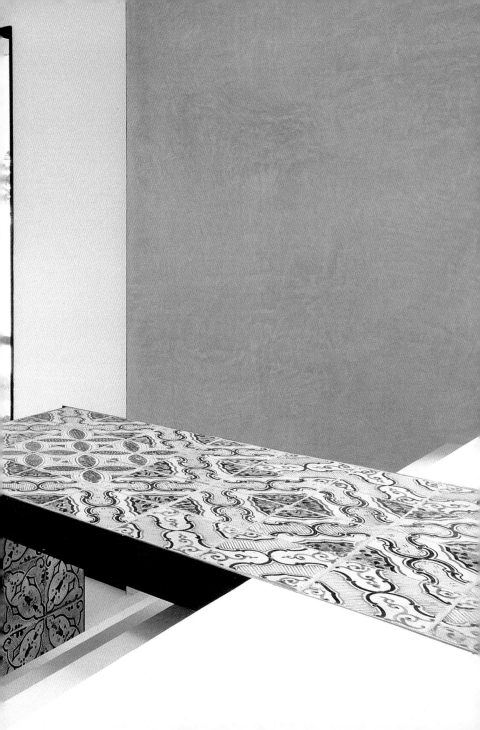

68/69 Hanne Kjærholm's deceased husband Poul designed the "PK33" stools. *Les tabourets « PK33 » sur la terrasse de Hanne Kjærholm ont été dessinés par son défunt mari Poul.* Die »PK33«-Hocker auf Hanne Kjærholms Terrasse entwarf ihr verstorbener Gatte Poul.

70/71 In the living area "PK31/2" sofas are placed on opposite sides of a Moroccan carpet. *Dans le séjour, deux canapés « PK31/2 » se font face sur un tapis marocain.* Im Wohnbereich stehen sich zwei »PK31/2«-Sofas auf einem marokkanischen Teppich gegenüber.

72/73 The bookshelves behind Hanne Kjærholm's desk are by Mogens Koch. *La bibliothèque, derrière le bureau de Hanne Kjærholm, est de Mogens Koch.* Die Bücherregale hinter Hanne Kjærholms Arbeitstisch stammen von Mogens Koch.

74/75 The throw on the bed in Hanne Kjærholm's bedroom was hand made in Mexico. *Un couvre-lit fait main au Mexique dans la chambre lambrissée de Hanne Kjærholm.* Der Bettüberwurf im Schlafzimmer von Hanne Kjærholm wurde in Mexiko handgefertigt.

76/77 Todd Saunders and Tommie Wilhelmsen maintain a deliberately minimalist style in their bedroom. *Todd Saunders et Tommie Wilhelmsen veulent une chambre de style minimaliste.* Todd Saunders und Tommie Wilhelmsen halten ihr Schlafzimmer bewusst minimalistisch.

78/79 Vincent Van Duysen has placed "Greta" armchairs by Citterio on a Persian carpet. *Vincent Van Duysen a placé des fauteuils « Greta » de Citterio sur un tapis iranien.* Auf einem iranischen Teppich hat Vincent Van Duysen »Greta«-Sessel von Citterio platziert.

80/81 The surface around the bathtub extends to the bedside table, on which there is a sculpture from Botswana. *L'extrémité du meuble encastrant la baignoire fait office de table de nuit.* Die Wannenumrandung verlängert sich zum Nachttisch.

82/83 The sculpture on a table in Pierre Cardin's "Anthénéa" is reminiscent of a ship's anchor. *Dans l'« Anthénéa » de Pierre Cardin, l'objet sculpté sur une table évoque une ancre.* Die Skulptur auf einem Tisch in Pierre Cardins »Anthénéa« erinnert an einen Schiffsanker.

84/85 On Ibiza José Gandía-Blasco and Ramón Esteve designed a finca in purist style. *José Gandía-Blasco et Ramón Esteve ont créé une finca de style puriste à Ibiza.* Auf Ibiza schufen José Gandía-Blasco und Ramón Esteve eine Finca im puristischen Stil.

86/87 Three lamps from Santa & Cole are suspended above the table and chairs of iroko wood. *Trois luminaires de Santa & Cole sont suspendus au-dessus de la table et des chaises en bois d'iroko.* Über dem Tisch und den Stühlen aus Irokoholz hängen drei Lampen von Santa & Cole.

88/89 A strip of antique Vietri tiles runs around the living room of this villa in Positano. *Dans une villa de Positano un ruban de carreaux de Vietri anciens traverse le séjour.* Den Wohnraum einer Villa in Positano durchzieht ein Band aus antiken Vietri-Fliesen.

90/91 Lazzarini and Pickering designed the "Flying Sofa" two metres above the floor. *Installé à deux mètres au-dessus du sol, le « Flying Sofa » est une création des Lazzarini et Pickering.* Das »Flying Sofa« in zwei Meter Höhe ist ein Entwurf von Lazzarini und Pickering.

92/93 The red sofa in the villa was designed by Francesco Binfaré for Edra. *Dans la villa, le canapé rouge est une création de Francesco Binfaré pour Edra.* Das rote Sofa in der Villa gestaltete Francesco Binfaré für Edra.

94/95 Fiona Swarovski's house is 1940s – the Vietri floor tiles are original. *La maison de Fiona Swarovski date des années 1940 – les carreaux de sol de Vietri sont d'origine.* Fiona Swarovskis Haus entstand in den 1940ern – die Vietri-Bodenfliesen sind noch original.

96/97 Swarovski had the walls painted coral red and selected eclectic works of art. *Swarovski a fait peindre les murs rouge corail et choisi des œuvres d'art éclectiques.* Swarovski ließ die Wände korallenrot streichen und wählte eklektische Kunstwerke aus.

98/99 The tiles in the bathroom with its maritime decor take up the colour of the walls. *Les carreaux de la salle de bains au décor marin reprennent la teinte des murs.* Die Kacheln im mit maritimem Dekor verzierten Bad greifen den Farbton der Wände wieder auf.

100/101 For her house on Filicudi, Belquis Zahir designed the sofa with its cover of Indian cotton. *Dans sa maison de Filicudi, Belquis Zahir a conçu le canapé houssé de coton indien.* Für ihr Haus auf Filicudi entwarf Belquis Zahir das mit indischer Baumwolle bezogene Sofa.

102/103 A sculptural chair by the local artist Antonio stands in Zahir's rustic guest room. *Une sculpture-chaise d'Antonio, un artiste local, dans la chambre d'amis rustique de Zahir.* In Zahirs rustikalem Gästezimmer steht eine Stuhl-Skulptur des einheimischen Künstlers Antonio.

104/105 Christina von Rosen extended her small house in Portugal to include a guest room. *Christina von Rosen a ajouté une chambre d'amis à sa petite maison du Portugal.* Christina von Rosen erweiterte ihr kleines Haus in Portugal um ein Gästezimmer.

106/107 The kitchen tiles are from Morocco; the stool was hand made in the Algarve. *Les carreaux de cuisine viennent du Maroc ; le tabouret a été fabriqué à la main en Algarve.* Die Küchenfliesen sind aus Marokko; der Hocker entstand in Handarbeit an der Algarve.

108/109 For the Angelopoulos Alberto Pinto chose sofas shaped like pebbles. *Pour le salon des Angelopoulos, Alberto Pinto a choisi des canapés dont la forme évoque des galets.* Für die Angelopoulos wählte Alberto Pinto Sofas, deren Form an Kieselsteine erinnert.

110/111 Alberto Pinto imitates the colours of the sea in his interior. *Les teintes bleu et blanc choisies par Alberto Pinto pour l'interieur imitent celles de la mer.* Die Farben des Meeres hallen auch im Innern wieder.

112/113 In the charming guest house, every room was painted in a different shade of blue. *Dans le charmant pavillon d'amis, chaque pièce a été peinte dans un autre ton de bleu.* Im charmanten Gästehaus wurde jeder Raum in einem anderen Blauton gestrichen.

114/115 Lisa Perry installed 14 "Bubble" lamps by George Nelson over the table. *Au-dessus de la table, Lisa Perry a fixé 14 lampes «Bubble» de George Nelson.* Über dem Tisch installierte Lisa Perry 14 »Bubble«-Lampen von George Nelson.

116/117 A colourful oil painting by Frank Stella on the wall above sofas by Tony Ingrao. *Une huile aux vives couleurs de Frank Stella est suspendue au-dessus de canapés de Tony Ingrao.* Ein farbenfrohes Ölgemälde von Frank Stella an der Wand über Sofas von Tony Ingrao.

118/119 Photos by Rineke Dijkstra decorate the Ganeks' house in the Hamptons. *Des photographies de Rineke Dijkstra décorent la maison des Ganek à Hampton.* Fotos von Rineke Dijkstra zieren das Haus der Ganeks in den Hamptons.

120/121 Chairs of wood and leather are grouped around George Nakashima's table. *Autour de la table de George Nakashima, des chaises en bois et cuir.* Um den Tisch von George Nakashima gruppieren sich Holz- und Lederstühle.

122/123 Chairs by Charlotte Perriand in Alan Wanzenberg's Ocean House. *Chaises de Charlotte Perriand dans la Ocean House d'Alan Wanzenberg.* Stühle von Charlotte Perriand in Alan Wanzenbergs Ocean House.

124/125 The simple pine bed in Bay House was designed by Alan Wanzenberg himself. *À Bay House, Alan Wanzenberg a conçu lui-même le lit tout simple en bois de pin.* Das schlichte Bett im Bay House entwarf Alan Wanzenberg selbst aus Kiefernholz.

126/127 For a house on Martha's Vineyard, Paula Perlini chose chairs by Louis J. Solomon. *Paula Perlini a choisi des chaises de Louis J. Solomon pour une maison de Martha's Vineyard.* Paula Perlini wählte für ein Haus auf Martha's Vineyard Stühle von Louis J. Solomon.

128/129 Furniture made of bamboo and sea grass underlines the informal style. *Des meubles en bambou et en zostère tressée soulignent le style décontracté de la maison de plage.* Möbel aus Bambus und Seegras unterstreichen den zwanglosen Stil des Strandhauses.

130/131 Bright flowers, loosely arranged, bring the colours of the natural surroundings into the house. *Des bouquets multicolores sans apprêt font entrer les couleurs de la nature ambiante dans la maison.* Bunte Blumen bringen die Farben der umliegenden Natur ins Innere.

132/133 The screen in the house by Jorge Pardo for the Reyes contrasts with the tiles. *Dans la maison des Reyes, par Jorge Pardo, le revêtement mural ajouré contraste avec les carreaux.* Das Gitter im von Jorge Pardo entworfenem Haus der Reyes kontrastiert mit den Fliesen.

134/135 Chairs by Eames complement the kitchen furniture of laminated cedarwood. *Les meubles de cuisine en cèdre laminé rencontrent avec bonheur les chaises d'Eames.* Die Küchenmöbel aus laminiertem Zedernholz werden durch Stühle von Eames ergänzt.

136/137 The furniture in the house in Iporanga is designed by Laura O. *Dans la maison à Iporanga, les meubles ont été dessinés par Laura O.* Die Möbel in dem Haus in Iporanga sind Designs von Laura O.

138/139 The vintage occasional table is by Grete Jalk. *La table basse vintage est de Grete Jalk.* Der Vintage-Beistelltisch ist ein Entwurf Grete Jalks.

140/141 Stairs of acacia wood are the focal point of Daan Nelemans' house in Costa Rica. *Un escalier en bois au cœur de la maison de Daan Nelemans au Costa Rica.* Eine Treppe aus Akazienholz bildet den Mittelpunkt von Daan Nelemans Haus in Costa Rica.

142/143 A papaya and shells lie on a coffee table that was made locally. *Une papaye et des coquillages sur une table basse fabriquée dans la région.* Auf einem Sofatisch, der in der Region gefertigt wurde, liegen eine Papaya und Muscheln.

144/145 The upholstery of the sofa in Hugo Ramasco's house in Uruguay is covered with sailcloth. *Chez Hugo Ramasco, en Uruguay, le canapé est recouverts de toile à voile.* Das Sofa in Hugo Ramascos Haus in La Pedrera in Uruguay ist mit Segeltuch bezogen.

146/147 For the open kitchen Hugo Ramasco chose a work surface of polished concrete. *Pour la cuisine ouverte, Hugo Ramasco a choisi un plan de travail en béton poli.* Für die offene Küche wählte Hugo Ramasco eine Arbeitsfläche aus poliertem Beton.

148/149 A cement fish and two iron candle holders adorn the fireplace. *Un poisson en ciment et deux chandeliers de fer décorent la cheminée.* Den Kamin zieren ein Fisch aus Zement und zwei Kerzenleuchter aus Eisen.

150/151 The fish in Michel Grether's home in Punta del Este was caught by a friend of his grandfather. *À Punta del Este, un ami du grand-père de Michel Grether a attrapé le poisson.* Den Fisch bei Michel Grether in Punta del Este fing ein Freund seines Großvaters.

152/153 Ken Crosson placed chairs by Riccardo Blumer around a table that he designed himself. *Autour de la table qu'il a dessinée, Ken Crosson a placé des chaises de Riccardo Blumer.* Um den selbst entworfenen Tisch stellte Crosson Stühle von Riccardo Blumer.

154/155 The tub can be rolled out of the house; the water drains off through the wooden planking. *La baignoire peut être avancée dehors ; l'eau s'écoule à travers les planches.* Die Wanne lässt sich ins Freie rollen; das Wasser fließt durch die Holzplanken ab.

"Night was coming on and the islands were looming up in the distance, always floating above the water, not resting upon it..."

Henry Miller, *The Colossus of Maroussi*

« La nuit tomba, et les îles devinrent visibles dans le lointain, elles planaient au-dessus de l'eau, elles ne la touchaient pas... »

Henry Miller, *Le colosse de Maroussi*

»Die Dunkelheit brach herein, und die Inseln wurden in der Ferne sichtbar, sie schwebten über dem Wasser, sie berührten es nicht ...«

Henry Miller, *Der Koloß von Maroussi*

DETAILS

Détails   Details

163 Tea time with a service by Grethe Meyer on a Poul Kjærholm table. *Le thé est servi dans une vaisselle de Grethe Meyer sur une table de Poul Kjærholm.* Teestunde mit einem Service von Grethe Meyer auf einem Poul-Kjærholm-Tisch.

164 The tables on Hanne Kjærholm's terrace were made from steel and granite. *Les tables de terrasse de Hanne Kjærholm ont été fabriquées en acier et granit.* Hanne Kjærholms Terrassentische wurden aus Stahl und Granit gefertigt.

165 A painting by Arne Haugen Sørensen in the dining room of the Kjærholms. *Un tableau de Arne Haugen Sørensen est accroché dans la salle à manger.* Im Esszimmer der Kjærholms hängt ein Bild von Arne Haugen Sørensen.

166 José Gandía-Blasco's home in Ibiza has a tub sunk into the floor. *José Gandía-Blasco à Ibiza, possède une baignoire encastrée dans le sol.* José Gandía-Blasco auf Ibiza besitzt eine im Boden versenkte Wanne aus Beton.

168 On board of the "Anthénéa", which Cardin has furnished in 1970s style. *À bord de l'« Anthénéa » que Cardin a aménagée dans le style des années 1970.* An Bord der »Anthénéa«, die Cardin im Stil der 1970er eingerichtet hat.

169 The main door of fibreglass can be opened hydraulically. *La porte en fibres de verre est dotée d'un système de levage hydraulique.* Die Fiberglastür lässt sich hydraulisch öffnen.

170 Belquis Zahir converted an old bread oven into a shower cubicle. *Belquis Zahir a transformé un vieux four en cabine de douche.* Belquis Zahir funktionierte einen alten Backofen zur Duschkabine um.

172 Balquis Zahir's veranda in the typical Aeolian style has a built-in bench. *Sur la véranda de Balquis Zahir, un canapé maçonné dans le plus pur style éolien.* Das gemauerte Sofa steht auf Balquis Zahirs Veranda im typisch äolischen Stil.

173 Paul Barthemely used simple petroleum lamps for outside lighting. *Chez Paul Barthemely, de simples lampes à pétrole pour éclairer dehors.* Bei Paul Barthemely dienen einfache Petroleumlampen als Außenbeleuchtung.

175 Gianna and Theodore Angelopoulos' terrace looks out over the sea of Mykonos. *La terrasse de Gianna et Theodore Angelopoulos s'ouvre sur la mer de Mykonos.* Die Terrasse der Angelopoulous zeigt aufs Meer vor Mykonos.

176 A female nude decorates the wall along Gianna and Theodore Angelopoulos' stairs. *Un nu féminin sur le mur de l'escalier, chez Gianna et Theodore Angelopoulos.* Ein weiblicher Akt ziert die Wand bei Gianna und Theodore Angelopoulos.

177 Tables and chairs in the simple style of the Cyclades. *Sur la véranda, Georges Evripiotis a disposé des tables et des chaises montrant le style sobre des Cyclades.* Tische und Stühle im schlichten Stil der Kykladen.

179 The decorative screen in the Reyes' house was designed by Jorge Pardo. *Les grilles décoratives chez les Reyes ont été déssinées par Jorge Pardo.* Die Ziergitter bei den Reyes wurden von Jorge Pardo entworfen.

180 A "Taraxacum" lamp by Flos hangs in Lisa Perry's kitchen. *Dans la cuisine de Lisa Perry, un luminaire « Taraxacum » de Flos éclaire la zone centrale.* In Lisa Perrys Küche hängt eine »Taraxacum«-Leuchte von Flos über dem zentralen Bereich.

181 The upper floor features Panton's "Fun 1 DM" lamps. *À l'étage supérieur on trouve des lampes « Fun 1 DM » de Panton.* In der oberen Etage findet man Pantons »Fun 1 DM«-Lampen.

183 The vintage chandelier in the Ganeks' foyer is by Verner Panton. *Le lustre vintage qui décore l'entrée des Ganek est de Verner Panton.* Die Vintage-Lampe im Foyer der Ganeks ist von Verner Panton.

184 Alan Wanzenberg's bathroom is panelled in wood. *La salle de bains d'Alan Wanzenberg est revêtue de boiseries.* In Alan Wanzenbergs Ocean House ist auch das Bad mit Holz verkleidet.

185 In the Ocean House a surfboard leans against the wall, ready for use. *Dans l'Ocean House une planche de surf est posée contre le mur, à portée de la main.* Im Ocean House lehnt ein Surfbrett griffbereit an der Wand.

187 Daan Nelemans finds decoration on the beach. *Daan Nelemans trouve ses ornements sur la plage.* Dekoration findet Daan Nelemans am Strand.

188 Hugo Ramasco takes his breaks on the veranda that surrounds the house. *Hugo Ramasco fait ses pauses sur la véranda qui fait le tour de sa maison.* Für Pausen nutzt Hugo Ramasco die Veranda, die sein Haus umgibt.

189 Ramasco prefers simple materials, such as pine and undyed fabrics. *Ramasco apprécie les matériaux sobres comme le bois ainsi que les tissus non teints.* Ramasco schätzt schlichte Materialien wie Holz und ungefärbte Stoffe.

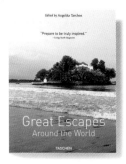
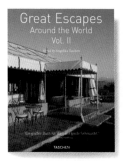

New Seaside Interiors
Ed. Angelika Taschen
Texts: Ian Phillips / Hardcover,
300 pp. / € 29.99 / $ 39.99 /
£ 29.99 / ¥ 5.900

**Great Escapes Around
the World**
Ed. Angelika Taschen
Hardcover, 720 pp. / € 39.99 /
$ 59.99 / £ 29.99 / ¥ 7.900

**Great Escapes Around
the World. Vol. 2**
Ed. Angelika Taschen
Hardcover, 672 pp. / € 39.99 /
$ 59.99 / £ 29.99 / ¥ 7.900

"**For those who are not yet beside the sea and have no hope of breathing salt air this year, here is solace in a shape to suit bibliophiles: TASCHEN's *New Seaside Interiors* ... every room, every page of the book opens up new prospects of the deep blue sea. Ideal for spending some time lounging and longing.**" —*Süddeutsche Zeitung*, Munich, on *New Seaside Interiors*

" Buy them all and add some pleasure to your life."